D1479619

THE BEST 50
MARTINIS

Jennifer L. Newens

BRISTOL PUBLISHING ENTERPRISES
San Leandro, California

Printed in the United States of America.

ISBN 1-55867-217-6

Cover design: Frank J. Paredes
Cover photography: John A. Benson
Food styling: Susan Massey

Martini Mania

Walk into any bar or upscale restaurant these days and you're likely to find, in addition to a wine list, a martini list, offering everything from a classic dry martini to a fanciful purple-colored martini flavored with blueberries. Whatever your preference, there's a martini for you.

The martini is regarded as a classy cocktail, evoking elegance, sophistication and an air of hedonism. Called the "King of Cocktails" by its devotees, the martini stands for prosperity and a devil-may-care attitude.

This book offers several varieties of martinis, from traditional and subdued to cutting-edge and crazy. There are also blank pages in the back of the book on which you can record your own martini creations.

A Little History

No one can say for sure where the martini originated, but its history has taken on the status of legend. Most agree that the martini was invented sometime in the latter part of the 19th century. Some claim that it was invented in San Francisco after the Gold Rush. Others assert that it was named after Martinez, California, where it was invented. Still others attribute its origin to New York City and its name to a bartender named Martini. Many other theories exist about the martini's beginning, and, it seems, each martini enthusiast has his or her own personal explanation.

Martinis first gained a foothold in American popular culture during Prohibition. During this period, gin replaced whiskey as America's favorite booze because it was far less complicated to bootleg. After Prohibition's repeal, martinis remained a standard, eventually entering their heyday in the 1950s during the Rat Pack's reign.

While gin was the original — and some argue the *only* — liquor for martinis, vodka gradually became a second option. This can be attributed to the James Bond novels and films from the 1960s, in which the hero asked for vodka martinis "shaken, not stirred."

Eventually martinis fell out of vogue, which some blame on a backlash to the 1980s decade of excess. But now, zealots young and old are driving a new martini mania. How do we explain the martini's recent surge in popularity? Perhaps it's from a longing for an easier era when having fun was as much a priority as working hard. Whatever the reason, martinis will no doubt linger as a symbol of the new millennium.

Famous Martini Drinkers

Humphery Bogart
George Burns
Winston Churchill
Noel Coward
F. Scott and Zelda Fitzgerald
Jackie Gleason
Ernest Hemingway
John F. Kennedy
Dorothy Parker
Franklin D. Roosevelt
Frank Sinatra and The Rat Pack
Mae West

Martini Ingredients

Martinis consist of 4 major ingredients. Each plays an essential part in creating a perfect martini.

- Gin or vodka
- Vermouth or other flavorings
- Garnishes, such as olives or lemon twists
- Ice

Since so few items make a martini, using top-quality ingredients is paramount. Use substandard products to mix a martini and you'll definitely notice a difference.

Gin

Gin is a clear, double-distilled, grain-based liquor flavored with juniper berries. It requires no aging, which is a good reason it was so popular during prohibition. Of the 3 types of gin manufactured today, London dry gin is most widely recognized and is the type used to make traditional dry martinis.

Vodka

Originally made in Russia from potatoes, vodka is now fabricated all over the world and is distilled from any grain, commonly wheat, corn and rye. By law, vodka must be distilled to be flavorless. However, manufacturers are now infusing herb and fruit flavors into their vodkas after distillation. Following are some examples of flavored vodkas that are currently available in stores:

- cinnamon
- coffee
- cranberry
- currant
- lemon
- orange
- peach
- pepper
- raspberry
- strawberry
- vanilla

Vermouth and Other Flavorings

Vermouth is wine that has been flavored with a special blend of herbs and spices. Dry white vermouth, also called French vermouth, is the type used to make classic martinis, but some early martini recipes added sweet red vermouth to the mixture. Vermouth can be found in many formulas, from dry to extra-dry, and is made in many countries, commonly France and Italy. Experiment with different types and manufacturers to find one that suits you. It is the amount of vermouth in a martini that determines its "dryness." An extremely dry martini would have merely a hint of vermouth as a flavoring.

Today, more and more bartenders are replacing the vermouth in their martinis with other liqueurs and aperitifs to create special signature martinis. Consult the *Glossary of Flavors*, pages 73 and 74, for a description of the flavorings used in this book's recipes.

Garnishes

Traditional garnishes for martinis are olives and lemon "twists." Cocktail onions garnish a variation of the martini called the *Gibson* (see page 30). These days, garnishes are anything-goes, ranging from anchovy-stuffed olives to pickled garden vegetables to edible flowers to just-shucked oysters.

The most common olives for martinis are Spanish-style green olives, sometimes stuffed with pimientos. Select only top-quality olives packed in glass jars. Look for them in specialty food stores or better supermarkets. Poor-quality olives will make a disappointing cocktail. For an extra-dry martini, some fans use *tipsy olives* (see page 9) instead of vermouth to give the gin or vodka just the right touch of flavor without adding additional vermouth.

Lemon twists are fashioned from the colored part of the fruit's peel (see page 9). Lemon twists are the standard, but other citrus peels can be used, especially to complement a martini made with an infused flavored vodka.

For an elegant presentation, spear garnishes, such as olives or cocktail onions, in groups of 2 or 3 on toothpicks and place inside the martini glass. If you're really trying to impress someone, consider using fancy cocktail picks with decorative designs to spear olives, cocktail onions or other types of garnishes.

To make tipsy olives: Drain a jar of best-quality olives and rinse in a colander under cool running water. Rinse jar and replace olives. Pour vermouth into jar until all olives are submerged. Secure the lid on the jar and refrigerate for at least 1 week before using.

To make lemon twists: Wash a lemon with warm soapy water, rinse well and pat dry. Using a citrus stripper or vegetable peeler, run the tool over the surface of the fruit, removing just the colored part of the peel (the white pith tastes bitter). If necessary, cut the peel into long strips.

Ice

The quality of the ice you use will make or break your martini. Don't neglect this important ingredient. If using ice cube trays, wash them with hot soapy water and rinse them completely. Fill the trays with spring water or filtered water. Smell your freezer to detect any odors. You may wish to clean it and/or provide a fresh box of baking soda to prevent unwanted flavors from permeating the ice. If your ice comes from an automatic dispenser, make sure your freezer is clean and odor-free.

Crushed ice melts faster than ice cubes and will chill a martini more quickly, but it will also dilute the mixture faster. Just the right amount of dilution will make the best martini.

To crush ice cubes: Quickly process a few ice cubes with a blender until the right consistency is achieved. Or, place cubes in a heavy-duty locking plastic bag and break into pieces with a hammer.

A proper martini must be very cold. To achieve this, it is a good idea to chill all of the elements before you start.

Gin, vodka and vermouth can be stored in the freezer. The liquids will not freeze, due to their high alcohol content, but will become syrupy. You can use room-temperature alcohol, but it will melt the ice faster, resulting in a more diluted drink.

Glassware can be chilled in the refrigerator until you are ready to pour the drinks. Be sure that your refrigerator is clean and odor-free or you may detect an aroma on the glassware. To chill glassware quickly, carefully submerge it upside down in a container of ice and let stand for at least 1 minute.

For best results, make only the amount of martinis that will be consumed at one time. This will keep the mixture from warming and diluting too quickly.

Martini Equipment

A martini just isn't a martini unless it is served in its classic triangle-shaped glass perched on a long stem. Martini glasses can be found almost anywhere these days. A housewares store that sells good-quality barware is a good place to start your search. When selecting martini glasses, look for those made of glass or crystal. Since you will be using the best-quality ingredients to make your martinis, plastic martini cups just aren't appropriate.

If you prefer your martinis shaken, rather than stirred, invest in a good-quality stainless steel or glass martini shaker with a tight-fitting lid. A stainless steel shaker is a good choice because it will chill the mixture more quickly than glass. Do not purchase an inexpensive aluminum shaker or you will end up with a metallic-tasting cocktail.

If you prefer your martinis stirred, rather than shaken, there are many elegant cocktail pitchers on the market made of glass. Look for one with a matching long stirring rod. You can also use a clean glass container for mixing your concoctions. Be sure to use a glass or stainless steel stirring implement, rather than one made from aluminum.

A cocktail strainer is handy for straining out small pieces of ice that you don't want to end up in your glass. The best strainers have coils around the rims. Choose a strainer made from stainless steel, not aluminum. Look for cocktail strainers in any store that sells barware or in a liquor store.

A shot glass, which measures between 1 and 1.5 ounces, is a useful tool to have on hand when making cocktails. Look for one that has graduated measurements on the side for ease in measuring. After you get accustomed to mixing drinks, you will be able to estimate the amount of liquor poured by sight or feel.

Mixing Martinis

Ask a hundred martini fans how they prefer their cocktails and you will probably get a hundred different answers. One of the most hotly debated subjects is the method of mixing. This book provides 2 general methods, one for shaking martinis and one for stirring martinis. Decide for yourself which method you prefer.

To Make a Shaken Martini

1. Fill a cocktail shaker halfway with crushed ice.

2. Using your favorite recipe, add the gin or vodka, vermouth or other flavorings, and secure the lid on the shaker.

3. Shake the mixture vigorously but briefly. If using a stainless steel shaker, it will become so cold you almost can't stand to hold it. The longer you shake the cocktail, the more diluted it will be.

4. Using a cocktail strainer, strain the mixture into a chilled martini glass and garnish as desired.

To Make a Stirred Martini

1. Place a small amount of crushed ice in a cocktail pitcher.

2. Using your favorite recipe, add the gin or vodka, vermouth or other flavorings, and stir briefly with a stirring rod or long spoon (do not use aluminum). The longer you stir the cocktail, the more diluted it will be.

3. Carefully strain the mixture into a chilled martini glass and garnish as desired.

About the Recipes

The recipes in this book are written in parts, allowing you to make more than one drink at a time, if desired. For best results, make only the amount of drinks that will be consumed at one time.

For successful martini making, follow these 6 steps:

1. Determine how large you want your martini to be. Most martinis are between 1½ and 3 ounces.

2. Determine how much liquor constitutes a "part" by dividing the number of parts in your recipe by the number of ounces in your desired drink. For example, for a 3-ounce *Classic Gin Martini*, page 18, consisting of 8 parts gin and 1 part vermouth (9 parts total alcohol), divide 3 (ounces) by 9 (parts). For this recipe, 1 part is equal to approximately ⅓ ounce.

3. Determine the amount of ingredients you will need for your recipe by multiplying the number of parts by the size of the parts. For example, you will need about 2⅔ ounces of gin (8 parts x ⅓ ounce) and ⅓ ounce vermouth (1 part x ⅓ ounce) to make one *Classic Gin Martini* in the example above.

4. Determine the total amount of alcohol you will need by multiplying the number of drinks by the number of parts. For example, to make 3 *Classic Gin Martinis* in the example above, you will need 8 ounces of gin (2⅔ ounces x 3 servings) and 1 ounce of vermouth (⅓ ounce x 3 servings).

5. Select a mixing method on pages 14 or 15.

6. Follow the directions for your recipe and toast your success.

Classic Gin Martini

The proper ratio of gin to vermouth will forever be debated. Determine for yourself the ideal combination.

6-8 parts gin
1 part dry vermouth
crushed ice
olive or lemon twist for garnish

Shake or stir gin and vermouth with ice (see pages 14 or 15) and strain into a chilled martini glass. Garnish with olive or lemon twist.

Classic Vodka Martini

The only way to decide on your ideal ratio of vodka to vermouth is to practice making martinis. But don't practice too much in one night!

6-8 parts vodka
1 part dry vermouth
crushed ice
olive or lemon twist for garnish

Shake or stir vodka and vermouth with ice (see pages 14 or 15) and strain into a chilled martini glass. Garnish with olive or lemon twist.

Driest Martini

Every martini enthusiast has a pet theory for making dry martinis. At your home bar, pick one of the following options. Or, record your signature recipe on a blank page in the back of this book.

vermouth
1 part gin or vodka
crushed ice
olive or lemon twist for garnish

Pour a small amount of vermouth in a chilled martini glass and swirl to coat the sides. Discard vermouth. Shake or stir gin or vodka with ice (see pages 14 or 15) and strain into martini glass. Garnish with olive or lemon twist.

Variation: The Wave

Shake or stir gin or vodka with ice (see pages 14 or 15) and strain into a chilled martini glass. Wave bottle of vermouth over martini glass and garnish with olive or lemon twist.

Variation: Churchill's Martini

Shake or stir gin or vodka with ice (see pages 14 or 15) and strain into a chilled martini glass. Look at bottle of vermouth and garnish martini with olive or lemon twist.

Variation: Tipsy Olive Martini

Shake or stir gin or vodka with ice (see pages 14 or 15) and strain into a chilled martini glass. Omit vermouth and garnish with 1 to 3 *Tipsy Olives* (see page 9) speared on a toothpick or cock-tail pick.

Naked Martini

This martini is stripped down to its bare essentials.

1 part gin or vodka
crushed ice
olive or lemon twist for garnish

Shake or stir gin or vodka with ice (see pages 14 or 15) and strain into a chilled martini glass. Garnish with olive or lemon twist.

James Bond Martini

Attributed to Ian Fleming, the creator of the James Bond character, this version was called a Vesper in Fleming's novel Casino Royale. *Remember: To be authentic, this must be shaken rather than stirred.*

6 parts gin
2 parts vodka
1 part Lillet blanc
crushed ice
lemon twist for garnish

Shake gin, vodka and Lillet with ice (see page 14) and strain into a chilled martini glass. Garnish with lemon twist.

007 Martini

When James Bond transformed from novel hero to film hero, he began to request that his martinis be made only of vodka. But one thing remained the same — he preferred them "shaken, not stirred."

5 parts vodka
1 part extra-dry vermouth
crushed ice
lemon twist for garnish

Shake vodka and vermouth with ice (see page 14) and strain into a chilled martini glass. Garnish with lemon twist.

Indecision Martini

A bartender might look at you strangely if you ask for this, but gin AND vodka in a martini really do make a delicious cocktail.

2 parts gin
1 part vodka
splash dry vermouth or Lillet blanc
crushed ice
lemon twist or olive for garnish

Shake or stir gin, vodka and vermouth with ice (see pages 14 or 15) and strain into a chilled martini glass. Garnish with lemon twist or olive.

Half-and-Half Martini

Equal parts gin or vodka and vermouth make a perfectly balanced cocktail.

1 part gin or vodka
1 part dry vermouth
crushed ice
olive or lemon twist for garnish

Shake or stir gin or vodka and vermouth with ice (see pages 14 or 15) and strain into a chilled martini glass. Garnish with olive or lemon twist.

Wimpy Martini

Slightly sweet and pink in color, this one is for beginners.

3 parts gin or vodka
1 part sweet vermouth
crushed ice
lemon twist for garnish

Shake or stir gin or vodka and vermouth with ice (see pages 14 or 15) and strain into a chilled martini glass. Garnish with lemon twist.

Perfect Martini

It's unclear how this martini earned its name, but a formula for a martini made with dry and sweet vermouth nicknamed "perfect" can be found in many different sources.

8-10 parts gin
1 part dry vermouth
1 part sweet vermouth
crushed ice
olive or lemon twist for garnish

Shake or stir gin and vermouths with ice (see pages 14 or 15) and strain into a chilled martini glass. Garnish with olive or lemon twist.

Buckeye Martini

A black olive, instead of a green olive, as a garnish resembles the large nut-like seed of a horse-chestnut tree, familiarly known as a buckeye.

6-8 parts gin or vodka
1 part dry vermouth
crushed ice
black olive for garnish

Shake or stir gin or vodka and vermouth with ice (see pages 14 or 15) and strain into a chilled martini glass. Garnish with black olive.

Gibson

The invention of this martini variation is attributed, in some sources, to Charles Dana Gibson, creator of the Gibson girls.

6-8 parts gin or vodka
1 part dry vermouth
crushed ice
3 cocktail onions for garnish

Shake or stir gin or vodka and vermouth with ice (see pages 14 or 15) and strain into a chilled martini glass. Spear onions with a toothpick or cocktail pick and place in glass for garnish.

Something's Fishy Martini

Anchovies add an unusual, old-country-style flavor to a martini.

6 parts gin or vodka
1 part dry vermouth
crushed ice
anchovy-stuffed olive or anchovy fillet for garnish

Shake or stir gin or vodka and vermouth with ice (see pages 14 or 15) and strain into a chilled martini glass. Garnish with stuffed olive or anchovy.

Martini alla Primavera

Literally "spring-style" in Italian, "alla primavera" refers to the use of vegetables in recipes. For this curious martini, choose your favorite type of pickled vegetables, such as asparagus, green beans, onions, garlic, cherry tomatoes, carrots, sweet or hot peppers or tomatillos, as a garnish. An assortment of vegetables will be a conversation starter at a cocktail party.

6-8 parts gin or vodka
1 part dry vermouth
crushed ice
pickled vegetables for garnish

Shake or stir gin or vodka and vermouth with ice (see pages 14 or 15) and strain into a chilled martini glass. Garnish with pickled vegetables.

Spanish Martini

A dash of sherry gives a martini a Spanish flair.

1 part gin or vodka
crushed ice
splash sherry
lemon twist for garnish

Shake or stir gin or vodka with ice (see pages 14 or 15) and strain into a chilled martini glass. Add sherry and garnish with lemon twist.

Dirty Martini

Olive brine gives this martini a slightly cloudy appearance, hence the name "dirty."

6-8 parts gin or vodka
1 part dry vermouth
crushed ice
splash olive brine
olives for garnish

Shake or stir gin or vodka and vermouth with ice (see pages 14 or 15) and strain into a chilled martini glass. Add olive brine and garnish with olives.

Smoky Martini

Scotch has a slightly smoky aroma and flavor. Use single malt Scotch for an even more pronounced smoky smell and taste.

6 parts gin
1 part dry vermouth
crushed ice
splash Scotch whisky
lemon twist for garnish

Shake or stir gin and vermouth with ice (see pages 14 or 15) and strain into a chilled martini glass. Add Scotch and garnish with lemon twist.

Variation: Smokiest Martini
Substitute vodka for gin and single malt Scotch for vermouth. Omit Scotch whiskey.

Cajun Martini

This cocktail will remind you of the spicy food found in New Orleans, land of the Cajuns. Make is as hot as you can stand by adding hot pepper sauce.

6 parts gin or vodka
1 part dry vermouth
crushed ice
hot pepper sauce, such as Tabasco, to taste
jalapeño-stuffed olive or pickled jalapeño for garnish

Shake or stir gin or vodka and vermouth with ice (see pages 14 or 15) and strain into a chilled martini glass. Add hot pepper sauce and garnish with stuffed olive or jalapeño.

Peppercorn Martini

Enliven a martini with peppercorns in 2 guises.

6 parts pepper-flavored vodka
1 part dry vermouth
crushed ice
rinsed green peppercorns for garnish

Shake or stir vodka and vermouth with ice (see pages 14 or 15) and strain into a chilled martini glass. Garnish with peppercorns.

New York Martini

The origin of this drink can be traced to the New York metropolitan area. Like most cocktails, the actual inventor and location is debated.

6 parts gin
1 part dry vermouth
crushed ice
splash orange juice
lemon twist for garnish

Shake or stir gin and vermouth with ice (see pages 14 or 15) and strain into a chilled martini glass. Add orange juice and garnish with lemon twist.

Kir Martini

Crème de cassis, French black currant liqueur, is used to make the French-style white wine cocktail called a Kir. Here it is used to make a classy variation of a martini.

3 parts currant-flavored vodka
1 part Lillet blanc
crushed ice
splash crème de cassis liqueur
lemon twist for garnish

Shake or stir vodka and Lillet with ice (see pages 14 or 15) and strain into a chilled martini glass. Add crème de cassis and garnish with lemon twist.

Parisian Martini

Parisians like to drink Dubonnet before dinner as an aperitif.
Combined with icy vodka and served in an elegant martini glass,
this cocktail is suitable for any festive event.

1 part vodka
crushed ice
splash Dubonnet red
lemon twist for garnish

Shake or stir vodka with ice (see pages 14 or 15) and strain into a chilled martini glass. Add Dubonnet and garnish with lemon twist.

French-Style Martini

Popular in France as a before-dinner drink, Lillet adds a refreshing, slightly sweet accent to a chilly vodka cocktail.

1 part vodka
crushed ice
splash Lillet blanc
lemon twist for garnish

Shake or stir vodka with ice (see pages 14 or 15) and strain into a chilled martini glass. Add Lillet and garnish with lemon twist.

Martini Aperitif

Campari, vodka and lime zest look elegant served in a decorative martini glass.

6 parts vodka
1 part Campari
crushed ice
lime twist for garnish

Shake or stir vodka and Campari with ice (see pages 14 or 15) and strain into a chilled martini glass. Garnish with lime twist.

Blue Yonder Martini

You can use regular curaçao for this drink, too, but blue curaçao turns a martini a mysterious sky-blue color.

4-6 parts gin or vodka
1 part blue curaçao
crushed ice
lemon twist for garnish

Shake or stir gin or vodka and curaçao with ice (see pages 14 or 15) and strain into a chilled martini glass. Garnish with lemon twist.

Ginger Martini

Ginger liqueur and crystallized ginger lend an intriguing, spicy flavor to this cocktail.

1 part vodka
crushed ice
splash ginger liqueur
crystallized ginger piece for garnish

Shake or stir vodka with ice (see pages 14 or 15) and strain into a chilled martini glass. Add ginger liqueur and garnish with crystallized ginger.

Fresh Air Martini

You won't need to take a breath mint after sipping this refreshing cooler.

6 parts vodka
1 part white crème de menthe liqueur or peppermint schnapps
crushed ice
peppermint candy or fresh mint sprig for garnish

Shake or stir vodka and crème de menthe with ice (see pages 14 or 15) and strain into a chilled martini glass. Garnish with peppermint candy or mint sprig.

Cinnamon Martini

Cinnamon schnapps is very strong, so take care when adding it to your cocktail. Drink this right away or the red hots will dissolve and turn the drink a pink color. For an elegant variation, use Goldschlager brand cinnamon schnapps instead of regular cinnamon schnapps. Its flecks of gold leaf will replace the red hot candies as a sophisticated garnish.

1 part vodka
crushed ice
dash cinnamon schnapps
red hot candies for garnish

Shake or stir vodka with ice (see pages 14 or 15) and strain into a chilled martini glass. Add cinnamon schnapps and garnish with red hots.

Peachy Keen Martini

During peach season, cut ripe peaches into slender wedges and use them to garnish this fruity concoction.

1 part regular or peach-flavored vodka
crushed ice
splash peach schnapps
peach slice or lemon twist for garnish

Shake or stir vodka with ice (see pages 14 or 15) and strain into a chilled martini glass. Add peach schnapps and garnish with peach slice or lemon twist.

Tropical Fling Martini

This combination of flavors is reminiscent of the oddly named cocktail "Sex on the Beach."

6 parts cranberry-flavored vodka
1 part peach schnapps
crushed ice
orange wheel for garnish

Shake or stir vodka and peach schnapps with ice (see pages 14 or 15) and strain into a chilled martini glass. Garnish with orange wheel.

Apple Pie Martini

Choose Calvados and this cocktail would be more aptly named "Tarte de Pommes Martini."

6 parts vodka
1 part Calvados or applejack
crushed ice
dash cinnamon schnapps
cinnamon stick for garnish

Shake or stir vodka and Calvados or applejack with ice (see pages 14 or 15) and strain into a chilled martini glass. Add cinnamon schnapps and garnish with cinnamon stick.

Lemon Martini

Serve this refreshing cocktail at a fete on a hot summer night.

5 parts lemon-flavored vodka
1 part Lillet blanc
crushed ice
lemon twist for garnish

Shake or stir vodka and Lillet with ice (see pages 14 or 15) and strain into a chilled martini glass. Garnish with lemon twist.

Variation: Citrus Twist Martini

Substitute citrus-flavored vodka for lemon-flavored vodka and add an orange twist as a garnish.

Lime Martini

You may wish to add a small amount of sugar or sweet liqueur to this bracing cocktail.

5 parts gin or vodka
1 part Rose's lime juice
crushed ice
lime twist for garnish

Shake or stir gin or vodka and lime juice with ice (see pages 14 or 15) and strain into a chilled martini glass. Garnish with lime twist.

Greyhound Martini

Vodka and grapefruit juice served on the rocks is called a Greyhound. Well-chilled and strained into a martini glass, these ingredients form an elegant take on the standard.

1 part vodka
crushed ice
splash grapefruit juice
maraschino cherry with stem for garnish

Shake or stir vodka with ice (see pages 14 or 15) and strain into a chilled martini glass. Add grapefruit juice and garnish with cherry.

Big Berry Martini

Add more or less Chambord to this cocktail, depending on how sweet and how pink you want it to be.

1 part gin or vodka
crushed ice
splash Chambord liqueur
lemon twist for garnish

Shake or stir gin or vodka with ice (see pages 14 or 15) and strain into a chilled martini glass. Add Chambord and garnish with lemon twist.

Raspberry Martini

Raspberries in 3 forms combine in a sweet-dream-of-a-cocktail.

5 parts raspberry-flavored vodka
1 part framboise liqueur
crushed ice
fresh raspberries for garnish

Shake or stir vodka and framboise with ice (see pages 14 or 15) and strain into a chilled martini glass. Garnish with raspberries.

Raspberry-Vanilla Martini

A pair of favorite dessert flavors combine effortlessly and elegantly in a cocktail that is not too sweet.

5 parts raspberry-flavored vodka
1 part vanilla-flavored vodka
crushed ice
vanilla bean or fresh raspberries for garnish

Shake or stir vodkas with ice (see pages 14 or 15) and strain into a chilled martini glass. Garnish with vanilla bean or raspberries.

Strawberry Martini

To impress your guests, choose plump, bright-red berries to garnish this drink.

5 parts strawberry-flavored vodka
1 part sweet vermouth or Lillet blanc
crushed ice
fresh strawberry for garnish

Shake or stir vodka and vermouth or Lillet with ice (see pages 14 or 15) and strain into a chilled martini glass. Garnish with strawberry.

Cherry Martini

When life seems like a bowl of pits, add some cherries to the mix in the form of a calming icy-cold cocktail.

5 parts vodka
1 part kirschwasser
crushed ice
long-stemmed cherry for garnish

Shake or stir vodka and kirschwasser with ice (see pages 14 or 15) and strain into a martini glass. Garnish with cherry.

Cranberry Martini

Gin and vodka are both delicious in this striking red concoction.

5 parts gin or vodka
1 part cranberry juice cocktail
crushed ice
fresh cranberry, lemon twist or orange twist for garnish

Shake or stir gin or vodka and cranberry juice with ice (see pages 14 or 15) and strain into a chilled martini glass. Garnish with cranberry, lemon twist or orange twist.

Variation: Cranberry-Orange Martini

Substitute orange-flavored vodka for gin or regular vodka. Garnish with orange twist.

Triple Orange Martini

Choose curaçao, Triple Sec, Cointreau, or any number of orange liqueurs instead of Grand Marnier. Sampled side by side, you'll notice a marked difference in the flavors of the liqueurs.

5 parts orange-flavored vodka
1 part Grand Marnier or other orange liqueur
crushed ice
orange twist for garnish

Shake or stir vodka and Grand Marnier with ice (see pages 14 or 15) and strain into a chilled martini glass. Garnish with orange twist.

Orange-Coffee Martini

This cocktail is a good choice for a late-night get-together.

5 parts coffee-flavored vodka
1 part Grand Marnier or other orange liqueur
crushed ice
chocolate-covered coffee beans or orange twist for garnish

Shake or stir vodka and Grand Marnier with ice (see pages 14 or 15) and strain into a chilled martini glass. Garnish with coffee beans or orange twist.

Mocha Martini

Chocolate and coffee flavors complement each other nicely. Choose dark instead of white crème de cacao for a deep, mysterious color and slightly fuller-bodied feel.

5 parts coffee-flavored vodka
1 part white or dark crème de cacao liqueur
crushed ice
chocolate-covered coffee beans for garnish

Shake or stir vodka and crème de cacao with ice (see pages 14 or 15) and strain into a chilled martini glass. Garnish with coffee beans.

Chocolate Martini

Currently this drink is all-the-rage at bars throughout San Francisco. Each bartender has his or her own secret formula.

6 parts regular or vanilla-flavored vodka
1 part white or dark crème de cacao liqueur
crushed ice
chocolate curls, chocolate kiss or
maraschino cherry with stem for garnish

Shake or stir vodka and crème de cacao with ice (see pages 14 or 15) and strain into a chilled martini glass. Garnish with chocolate curls, chocolate kiss or cherry.

Nutty Martini

Many liqueurs on the market are flavored with nuts. Choose your personal favorite.

6 parts vodka
1 part Frangelico or amaretto liqueur
crushed ice
hazelnuts or almonds for garnish

Shake or stir vodka and Frangelico or amaretto with ice (see pages 14 or 15) and strain into a chilled martini glass. Garnish with hazelnuts or almonds.

Licorice Martini

If you're in an Italian sort of mood, choose sambucca for this drink. If you're feeling French-like, Pernod is your choice.

5 parts vodka
1 part sambucca liqueur or Pernod
crushed ice
black licorice candy or lemon twist for garnish

Shake or stir vodka and sambucca or Pernod with ice (see pages 14 or 15) and strain into a chilled martini glass. Garnish with licorice candy or lemon twist.

Almost Virgin Martini

Teetotalers can still look elegant when their drinks are served in long-stemmed martini glasses.

4 parts spring water
1 part dry or sweet vermouth
crushed ice
olive or lemon twist for garnish

Shake or stir water and vermouth with ice (see pages 14 or 15) and strain into a chilled martini glass. Garnish with olive or lemon twist.

_____

_____

_____

_____

_____

_____

_____

_____

_____

_____

_____

_____

_____

_____

_____

_____

_____

_____

_____

_____

_____

_____

_____

_____

_____

_____

_____

_____

_____

_____

_____

_____

_____

_____

_____

_____

_____

_____

_____

My Martinis

_____

_____

_____

_____

_____

_____

_____

_____

_____

_____

—————————————————————

—————————————————————

—————————————————————

—————————————————————

—————————————————————

—————————————————————

—————————————————————

—————————————————————

—————————————————————

—————————————————————

Glossary of Flavors

applejack: wood-aged American apple brandy

amaretto: almond liqueur

Calvados: apple brandy made in Normandy, France

Chambord: French raspberry liqueur

cinnamon schnapps: strong cinnamon-flavored liquor

crème de cassis: black currant liqueur

crème de cacao: chocolate-flavored liqueur

crème de menthe: mint-flavored liqueur

curaçao: liqueur made from bitter oranges on the island of Curaçao

Dubonnet red: sweet wine fortified with herbs and other flavorings, usually consumed as an *aperitif* (a drink designed to stimulate the appetite)

framboise: French raspberry brandy

Frangelico: hazelnut liqueur

Grand Marnier: French orange liqueur

grenadine: pomegranate-flavored syrup

kirschwasser: cherry brandy

Lillet blanc: a blend of wine, fruits, herbs and other flavorings from France, usually consumed as an aperitif (a drink designed to stimulate the appetite); it can also be called blonde Lillet

peach schnapps: strong peach-flavored liquor

peppermint schnapps: strong peppermint-flavored liquor

Pernod: licorice- (anise) flavored liqueur from France

sambucca: licorice- (anise) flavored liqueur from Italy

single malt Scotch: distilled malt-based liquor with a pronounced smoky flavor

sweet vermouth: fortified white wine flavored with herbs and spices; it's red in color and is usually consumed as an *aperitif* (a drink designed to stimulate the appetite)

Selected Bibliography

Berk, Sally Ann. *The Martini Book*. New York: Black Dog & Leventhal, 1997.

Coconut Grove Media. Http://www.wco.com. 1997.

Epicurious. Http://www.epicurious.com. 1997.

Ketel One vodka. Http://www.ketelone.com

Martini & Rossi vermouth. Http://www.bacardi.com

Martini Madness. Boynton Beach, FL: The American Cooking Guild, 1997.

Miller, Anistatia R. and Brown, Jared M. *Shaken Not Stirred: A Celebration of the Martini*. New York: HarperCollins, 1997.

Tanqueray gin. Http://www.tanqueray.com

The New York Times on the Web. Http://www.nytimes.com. 1998.

The Salt Lake Tribune. Http://www.sltrib.com. 1996.

Shaken not Stirred. Http://www.axionet.com/key/martinis.html

Index